THE SECRET LIFE OF A
SNOWFLAKE

AN UP-CLOSE LOOK AT THE ART & SCIENCE OF SNOWFLAKES

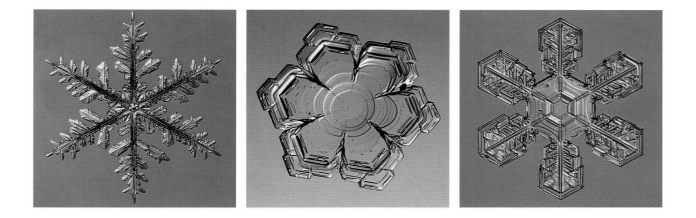

Kenneth Libbrecht

Voyageur Press

First published in 2009 by Voyageur Press, an imprint of MBI
Publishing Company, 400 First Avenue North, Suite 300,
Minneapolis, MN 55401 USA

Voyageur Press titles are also available at discounts in bulk quantity for industrial or sales-promotional use.
For details write to Special Sales Manager at MBI Publishing Company, 400 First Avenue North, Suite 300,
Minneapolis, MN 55401 USA.

To find out more about our books, visit us online at www.voyageurpress.com.

Library of Congress Cataloging-in-Publication Data

Libbrecht, Kenneth George.
 The secret life of a snowflake : an up-close look at the art and science of
snowflakes / Kenneth Libbrecht.
    p. cm.
 ISBN 978-0-7603-3676-2 (hb w/ jkt)
 1. Snowflakes—Juvenile literature. 2. Ice crystals—Growth—Juvenile
literature. I. Title.
 QC926.37.L53 2009
 551.57'841—dc22

                                          2009007892

Edited by Danielle Ibister
Design Manager: Katie Sonmor
Designed by Pauline Molinari

Printed by 1010 Printing International Ltd.
Yuanzhou, Guangdong, China
First printing October 2009

No snowflake ever falls in the wrong place.
—Chinese proverb

The wonder of snowflakes

Have you ever taken a close look at the falling snow?

Some days, when the weather is just right, the snow **crystals** look like tiny ice flowers. They float gently down and get caught in the tree branches.

A beautiful Vermont snowfall.

Photograph by Martha Macy

PHOTOGRAPHING SNOWFLAKES

I have an unusual hobby. I look at snowflakes under a microscope and take photographs of what I see. First I let the snow fall onto a blue collecting board. Then I look closely for interesting crystals.

When I spot one I like, I use a small paintbrush to carefully pick it up and place it onto a glass slide. Then I put the slide under my microscope and photograph the snowflake. I have taken thousands of pictures this way, of all kinds of snowflakes.

Each snowflake has its own unique design.
No two are exactly alike.

This page shows the sizes of some snowflakes when compared to a penny.

CLEAR AS ICE

Snowflakes are crystals of pure ice, which is clear and colorless. Seen through my microscope, each snowflake looks like a tiny piece of carved glass.

You need a microscope to see all the details in a snowflake. Looking with just your eyes, the bright edges of the crystals blur together. That is why the snowflakes on your sleeve look white.

COLORFUL SNOWFLAKES

When I photograph snowflakes, I like to shine colored lights though the ice from behind. The lights make the clear ice look colorful.

13

WHITE AS SNOW

When light hits a pile of snow, it bounces off all the tiny surfaces and edges of the ice crystals. The snow does not absorb much of the light. The sum of all the countless reflections makes a snowbank look bright white.

LIGHT MAKES WHITE

This picture shows small piles of salt, sugar, and crushed glass (from left to right). You may not know it, but salt and sugar are both clear and colorless, just like glass and ice.

Any pile of small, clear objects looks white. Salt, sugar, crushed glass, and snowflakes all look white because they reflect light instead of absorbing it.

THE SECRET LIFE OF A SNOWFLAKE

As a scientist, I try to understand how things work in the natural world. I especially like to study snowflakes.

How are snowflakes made? Why do they have such wonderful shapes? Why are they all so different? To answer these questions, we must look at what snowflakes are and how they form. We must learn the secret life of a snowflake!

THE CHANGING STATES OF WATER

The life of a snowflake begins with water. When you heat a pot of water on your stove, some of the water **evaporates** to become **water vapor** in the air. As the warm, moist air rises and cools, some of the water vapor **condenses.** It forms tiny drops of water called **droplets**. The water droplets are so small and light that they simply float in the air.

You cannot see water vapor in the air, but you can see the cloud of water droplets above a boiling pot. The cloud looks white because it is made from so many tiny droplets.

MAKING CLOUDS

You can see water evaporating and condensing outside on a much grander scale. Instead of a small pot of water, we have vast oceans and lakes. Instead of a stove, the sun provides the heat. Water in oceans and lakes evaporates to become water vapor in the air. The water vapor condenses into water droplets.

This is how clouds form. The clouds you see floating in the sky are made of countless numbers of tiny water droplets.

WHAT HOLDS UP THE CLOUDS?

Even a small cloud contains many tons of water, yet it simply floats through the air. This is possible because the cloud droplets are so tiny. Even the slightest wind will carry them.

A cloud droplet is about one hundred times smaller than a raindrop and a million times lighter. This drawing compares the sizes of a cloud droplet, a human hair, and a raindrop.

CLOUD
DROPLET

RAINDROP

HUMAN
HAIR

A cloud droplet freezes . . .

. . . and a snowflake is born.

THE BIRTH AND GROWTH OF A SNOWFLAKE

When the weather gets cold, the droplets inside a cloud start to freeze. As soon as a single droplet turns to ice, it begins growing into a snowflake.

Water vapor in the air condenses and freezes to add more ice to the newly born snowflake. As the snowflake grows, the droplets around it evaporate and shrink.

FALLING SNOWFLAKES

Snowflakes are not frozen raindrops. Instead they grow from water vapor that comes from evaporating cloud droplets. It takes about 100,000 tiny cloud droplets to make a single snowflake that is heavy enough to fall to Earth.

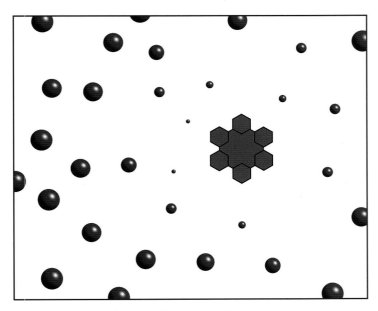

The snowflake grows larger . . .

. . . while the nearby cloud droplets evaporate away.

THE NUMBER SIX

Many snowflakes look like six-pointed stars. While snowflakes all have different shapes, you will never find one with four, five, seven, or eight branches.

Why six?

Even the tiniest cloud droplet contains trillions of **water molecules**. A water molecule is the smallest unit of water that can exist. You cannot see water vapor in the air because the separate water molecules are so small.

When water freezes into ice, the water molecules all line up in a pattern to make an ice crystal. The molecules always hook together to form small **hexagons**, which have six sides.

Snowflakes are shaped like hexagons because of the way the water molecules line up within the ice crystal.

AN ICE CRYSTAL

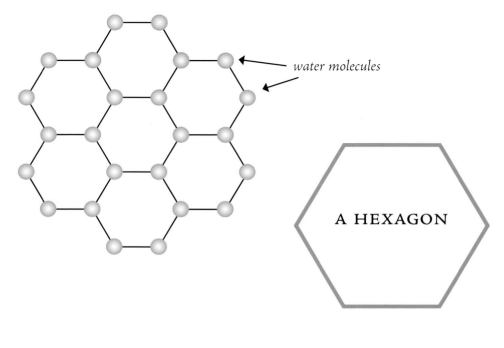

water molecules

A HEXAGON

How many hexagons can you find in these snowflakes?

Making hexagons

As more and more molecules attach to a growing snow crystal, they first fill in the rough spots on the surface. After a while, only smooth areas remain. These smooth surfaces are called **crystal facets**. The facets on an ice crystal make a hexagonal shape.

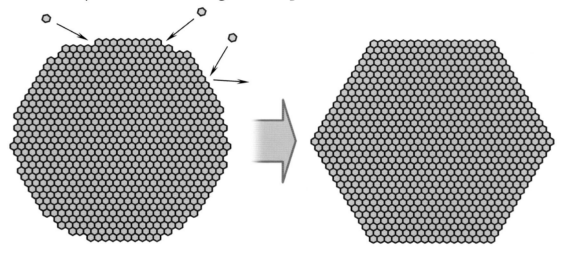

I grew these tiny snowflakes in my laboratory. Each is smaller than the width of a human hair. Such tiny snowflakes have very simple shapes.

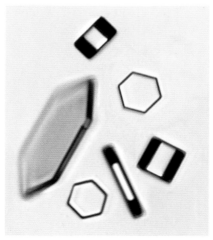

SALTY CUBES

Not all crystals are made of hexagons, because different kinds molecules stack differently. For example, the molecules that make up a crystal of salt stack up to form small squares. When a block of salt is ground up, it breaks into tiny cubes. You can see this shape if you look closely at what comes out of your salt shaker.

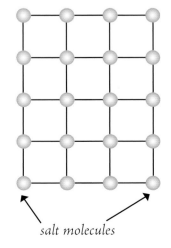

salt molecules

Branches and side branches

A snowflake grows larger as more water vapor in the air condenses and freezes onto it. The corners of the hexagon grow a bit faster than the sides because they stick out farther into the **humid** air. As the snowflake grows, branches sprout from the corners of the hexagon.

As the branches grow, they sprout side branches. With time, a fancy, star-shaped snowflake appears.

Large, star-shaped snowflakes always start out as small hexagons.

THE RIGHT WAY TO MAKE A PAPER SNOWFLAKE

Snowflakes have six branches. Use these steps to fold and cut a piece of paper to make a snowflake that looks like the real thing.

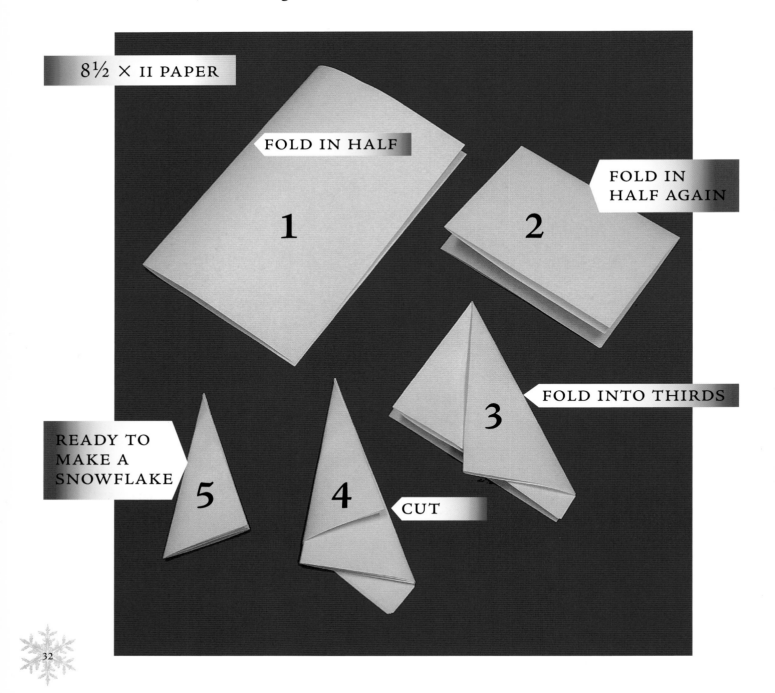

8½ × 11 PAPER

FOLD IN HALF

1

FOLD IN HALF AGAIN

2

FOLD INTO THIRDS

3

READY TO MAKE A SNOWFLAKE

5

4

CUT

Try making paper snowflakes that look like these real ones.

GROWING SNOWFLAKES

As a snowflake tumbles through the clouds, the temperature and humidity of the air around it change along the way. These changes affect how the ice crystal grows.

The final shape of a snowflake depends on the exact path it followed while it was growing. No two snowflakes are alike because each followed a different path through the clouds.

A snowflake

is born

and it grows

and tumbles

and falls

until it lands

on your sleeve.

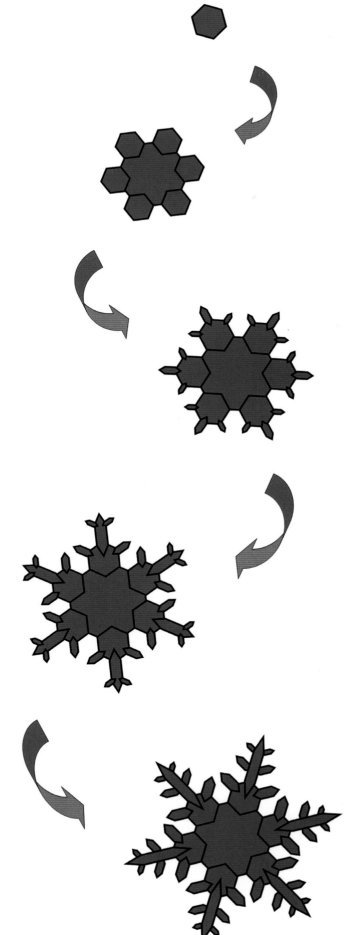

How many ways to make a snowflake?

I have figured out about how many different ways a snowflake can grow. The number is very large—larger than the total number of atoms in all the stars in all the galaxies in all of space! Even without looking at every snowflake, I can safely say that no two large, star-shaped snowflakes are exactly alike.

On the other hand, young, simple snowflakes cannot take as many different forms. I grow very simple snow crystals like these in my laboratory, and they often look alike.

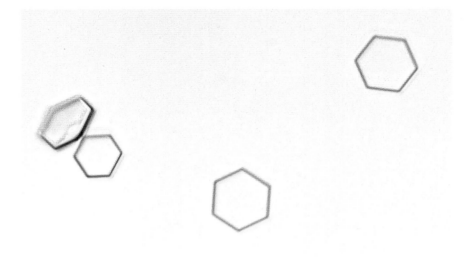

EQUAL ARMS ...

The six arms of a snowflake often look nearly identical.
All six branches grow the same because all six take the
same path through the clouds.

...Or not

But I also find many lopsided snowflakes on my collecting board. These shapes can form if the crystals bump or break while they are growing.

ICE FERNS

Some snowflakes have so many side branches that they look like tiny ice ferns. I have been in many snowfalls where nearly all the crystals looked like these.

This is one of the largest snow crystals I have ever seen. It is about half the size of a penny. It is quite a sight to see such giant ice flowers floating gently down all around!

Needles and pins

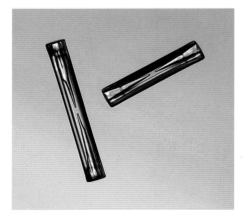

Not all snowflakes look like flowers or stars. I see many that are shaped like columns or thin **ice needles**. These types of snowflakes fall when the temperature is close to 23 degrees Fahrenheit (-5 degrees Celsius).

You may not always see it, but snow crystal columns have six sides. They have the same basic shape as a wooden pencil. This shape comes from the way the water molecules stack inside the crystal—the same reason star-shaped snowflakes have six arms.

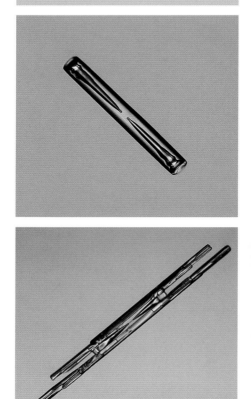

Sometimes I see the clouds dropping nothing but needle crystals. They look like short bits of hair on my sleeve.

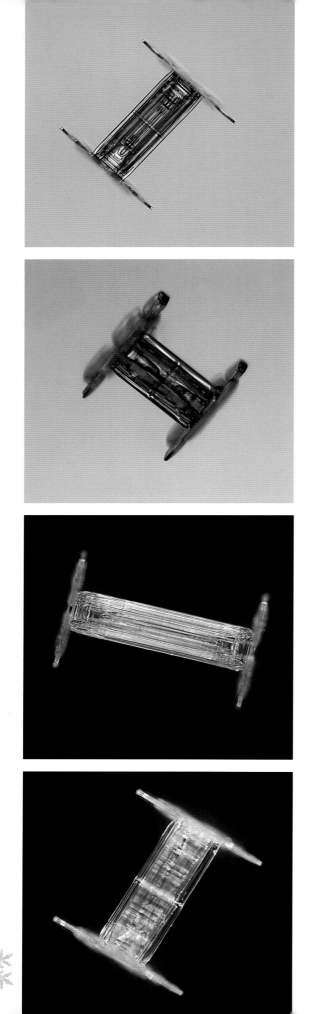

Capped columns

One of my favorite types of snowflake is called a **capped column**. It is a column with two plates on its ends, like an axle with two wheels.

Capped columns are often found during warmer snowfalls, when the temperature is just below freezing. Look for capped columns the next time it snows!

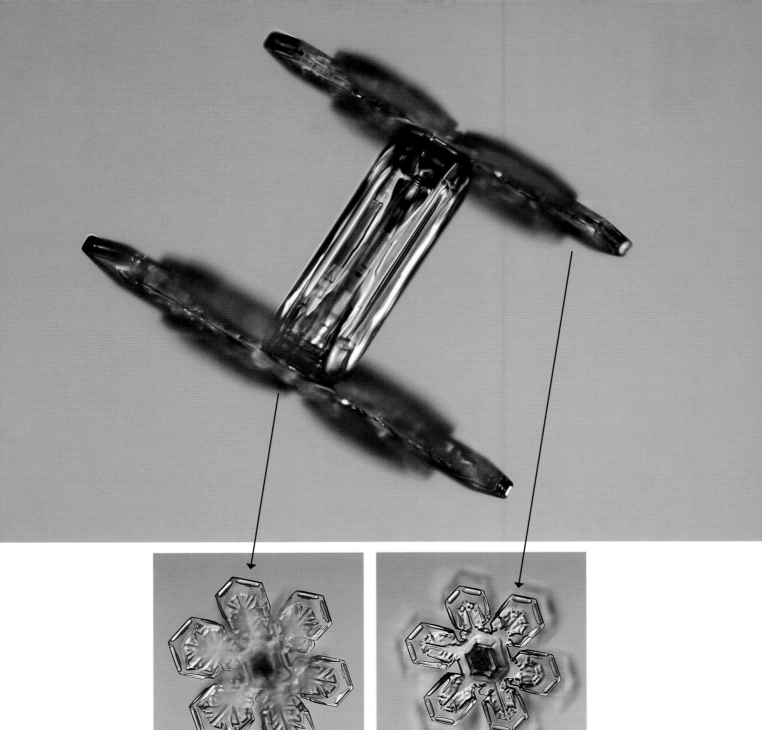

I first photographed this capped column from the side, which gave the top picture. Then I set it on end and focused on the bottom and top plates for the other two pictures.

Winter's secret beauty

The next time it snows, go outside with a magnifying glass and take a close look at the falling snowflakes. You may be amazed by what you find!

GLOSSARY

CAPPED COLUMN. A snowflake that is shaped like a column with two plates on its ends.

CONDENSATION. When water vapor turns into liquid water or ice.

CRYSTAL FACET. A smooth surface on a crystal.

CRYSTAL. A solid made of molecules lined up in a repeating pattern.

DROPLET. A tiny drop of water that is so small and light that it floats in the air.

EVAPORATION. When liquid water becomes water vapor.

HEXAGON. A shape that has six sides.

HUMIDITY. The amount of water vapor in the air.

ICE NEEDLE. A snowflake that is shaped like a needle or column.

WATER MOLECULE. The smallest unit of water that can exist.

WATER VAPOR. Water in gas form.

INDEX

About the Author and Photographer

Dr. Kenneth Libbrecht is a professor of physics at Caltech, where he studies how crystals grow. His books include *Ken Libbrecht's Field Guide to Snowflakes, The Art of the Snowflake,* and others. His latest news and views about snowflakes can be found at his website, www.SnowCrystals.com.